LIVING A LIFE OF SUCCESS

Fulfilling your dreams in the world of diversion

By

AMANDA ANDERSON

TABLE OF CONTENT

INTRODUCTION

Your success in life depends on you and you alone. It depends on your mindset and your self-discipline. To become successful isn't a day job. It takes persistence, consistency, passion, and self-denial of certain things.

There is no single measure of success, and certainly no single answer for how to be successful in life. Yet by looking at some of the habits of successful people, you can learn new tactics and strategies to implement in your own daily life. Cultivate and nurture these abilities, and over time you may find that you are better able to reach your goals and achieve the success you want in life.

Every day, hundreds of thousands of people look for ways to succeed in life. They keep looking for the formula for success. They look for freedom, money, early retirement, promotions, and praise, but they never find it. Many people unintentionally stumble upon this success formula, but even when they do, they fail to recognize it. They can see the secret there in front of them, but they shy away from it since it doesn't appear to be what they expected. Getting what you want: Everyone aspires to and works toward the success they have in mind. Success is incredibly tough for people to acquire; some did so through dedication and hard effort, whereas others didn’t achieve it. There is always a success story behind every successful person about how they achieved success and made their dreams come true.

WHAT ARE THE SECRETS TO SUCCESS

1. NEVER GIVE UP

The key to success is to never give up on your dreams of achievement. Some people fight and work incredibly hard to achieve their aspirations and goals, but when they encounter some sort of setback, they give up, stop trying, and believe they will never succeed. They gave up in a way even though they were practically guaranteed to achieve their objectives and goals. Failures can teach us and give us experience. Failures force you to make a lesson out of them. When you fail, alter the plan but leave the goals alone and begin working on it again with new plans and strategies.

2. BE EAGER TO LEARN

One of the secrets to success is to always learn and broaden your knowledge. Make it a habit to read various books that interest you if you want to succeed. This will broaden your knowledge. By reading a book every day, you can expand your knowledge and develop your creativity, both of which will aid you in achieving success. People that are successful consistently read books.

3. SHARE YOUR KNOWLEDGE

If you want success in life, you have to share your information and knowledge with other people. and help them with the knowledge you have. Live for others not only for yourself, be beneficial for others.

4. TAKE RISK

You must take chances if you want to succeed because success cannot be attained without them. It is analogous to someone who wants to be a successful businessperson but is unwilling to take a calculated risk by investing money in a venture. It is impossible to achieve success without taking a risk. To attain your objectives and goals, you must take risks.

5. DISCOVER YOUR POTENTIALS

You must first uncover who you are and what your secret talents and abilities are if you want to succeed in life. You must follow yourself about what you can do, what your talent and secret abilities are, rather than following trends, scopes, or other people. You must select the field for which you created it. Work on yourself to uncover your hidden talents and areas of interest so you can pursue what you love.

6. HARD WORK

Many successful people achieved their success due to hard-working. If you want to achieve success then work hard and dream big and never give up due to facing failures. Many people want to achieve their goals and make their dreams come true but they only say this and don't work hard for that, they cannot achieve success without hard work. Nothing can happen by sitting idle and only talking about your goals and dreams and not struggling and working hard for that. Success cannot come to you. you have to step forward toward success then the success will come to you.

7. FOCUS ON YOUR GOAL

The key to success is to put your attention on your objectives, aspirations, and desires because without them, you cannot succeed. Success is similar to trying to realize certain objectives or aspirations. Without any sort of goals and desires, success in life is meaningless, and you cannot accomplish your achievement. You must be aware of your aspirations and goals, as well as the steps necessary to fulfill them. And keep your attention on your ambitions, how you'll attain them, and what you need to do to get there.

LIVING A LIFE OF SUCCESS

Do you struggle to find a quiet moment during the day to unwind and kick your feet up? Are you pressed for time, under pressure, and prepared to give up? Why is it the case? Who is in charge of it? Why did we make it so challenging?

Simplify your life as a simple solution.

Whatever you consider being successful in life is a success. Maybe you're trying to figure out how to succeed so that you may have a flexible schedule or financial freedom.

Whatever you consider being successful in life is a success. Perhaps you want to figure out how to succeed so that you can have a flexible schedule or financial freedom.

Some may want to travel the world while others just want to pursue what they're passionate about. Being successful isn't necessarily about being rich or winning awards, it can also be about personal fulfillment.

If you had to design your perfect day, what would it look like?

Your reasons for wanting to master life skills will vary. Your spouse, parents, and friends could each have a different idea of what success is. But you don't need their definitions. Nothing will inspire you more than simmering wrath inside of you. The desire to succeed will motivate you to overcome challenges, put in a little more effort, and pursue happiness, which will help you lead a more fulfilling life.

How To Be Successful In Life

1. Create better goals

What's your big life purpose?

Maybe you define success as doing something to save endangered species of animals or to clean up the oceans.

How do you do it, then? Well, you need money, and that's where your money goal comes into play.

How much money are you going to need to help with those issues? Obtain a calculator and begin calculating the numbers.

Now you've got a specific goal, a date to achieve it, and a purpose for achieving it.

2. Stop looking for validation

You won't discover the answers to your questions about how to succeed in life among those around you. Unless everyone in your vicinity is a huge success.

You don't need permission from your parents, best friend, partner, or even your dog, to start a business. Live your own life. Stop relying on other people to confirm that you are headed in the right direction. Keep outside influences out of your mind.

3. Start living your dreams

Life success doesn't revolve around a miraculous turning point where everything comes together. It's about the insignificant intervals in between. times when you're content. times that you are savoring. You can start working on your web business during the evenings and weekends if that is your objective. You want everything and you want it now, I know what you're thinking.

But the truth is, unless you take those baby steps, you will know whether it’s something you want or something you think you want.

4. Start building your expertise

You don't have to start at the top, but you can work your way there. You will be astounded by your improvement in a year if you consistently set aside time each day to invest in it. Spend some time learning and experimenting with various marketing gimmicks if you manage an online store.

If you persevere for a year, you'll probably see that your sales have been increasing.

Write for a year, every day, if you're a writer. You'll probably notice that you've begun to build a devoted following by experimenting with various writing techniques and producing regular content. Developing your knowledge takes work. And your area of knowledge will assist you in discovering the solution to the problem of how to succeed.

5. Start doing

If you haven't done anything, you can't succeed. There isn't a sizable cash incentive for merely attending. You must invest the necessary time and effort into creating anything. The most prosperous individuals are all producers, after all.

Mark Zuckerberg created Facebook. Jeff Bezos created Amazon. Sara Blakely created Spanx.

And if you dedicate your life to creating, you could ultimately begin to understand what it takes to succeed. However, it does require patience and constant work.

After a long day at work, I know it's simpler to just turn on Netflix and switch off your brain, but the outcomes you desire come from keeping your brain active after work. by working harder than everyone else.

Finding success isn't about luck. It requires a great deal of courage and big thinking, as well as the motivation to overcome those fears that can keep you stuck in accepting smaller parcels of reward.
Success is within reach if you are willing to put in the work. But to do the right work, you must first learn the rules to success. It is not necessarily a destination but a journey that helps develop the skills and resources you need to thrive.

What are good rules for success in life — Success isn't mainly about achievement. It's about purpose, meaning, and contribution. There are many different tactics for how to be successful in life, but the strategy that works best for you may depend on what success means to you. There is no single right way to be successful. What works for you might not work for someone else.

What are the rules of success??

1. Always build a growth mindset. People who possess a fixed mindset believe that things such as intelligence are static and unchangeable.
2. Improve your emotional intelligence. Always pay attention and manage your emotions.
3. Always develop mental toughness. People who possess this mental strength see challenges as opportunities
4. Focus on intrinsic motivation. Challenge yourself, stay curious, and take control but don't fear competition
5. Always set achievable goals. Successful people know that they need to start by having attainable goals to achieve.

WHAT MAKES A PERSON SUCCESSFUL

How would you define a successful person?

If you want to bring success into your life, you should cultivate yourself just as you'd cultivate a garden for the best yield. The attributes here are shared by successful people everywhere, but they don't happen by accident or luck. They originate in habits, built a day at a time.

1. Successful people take responsibility for their actions. To be successful, you have to accept that you're responsible for your actions, your reactions, and ultimately your success and failures. This creates a mindset of empowerment and control.
2. Successful people keep a to-be list. This stems from knowing the importance of personal growth within the journey to success and becoming a person capable of achieving that success.
3. They focus on themselves. successful people focus on their personal growth and concentrate on their responsibility for success.

4. Successful people set goals. Thinking big and believing you can achieve them gives you something to strive for. It creates structure and it creates a game plan no matter how small the goals are.
5. Successful people do more than what was asked of them.

LIVING WITHOUT DISTRACTION

A distraction-free life might not always be possible, but creating an environment with less distraction, and distraction-free blocks of time will raise your level of engagement and lower stress and overwhelm. A distraction-free life is an art because you have to create it. It is intentional and made with purpose.

Ask yourself: how often did you lose concentration as a result of mundane distractions?

Distraction is a choice, Think of your life like a business, and you are the CEO. You decide what kind of "company" you want it to be.

The following are some of the most effective ways to cut out distractions in everyday life. Combined, these habits will ensure distraction-free living and bolster your work output.

1. Always ensure distracted-free surroundings. If it's your phone, put it somewhere else.
2. Always simplify your task. The idea is to give your task a simple definition, purpose, and time limit.
3. Be confident about what matters most. Trust your heart. You know what matters most. Defend it by giving it all of you.
4. Properly make use of your free time
5. Learn how to ignore. if things are not important and don't deserve our full

attention, just ignore it. You have better things to do and worry about.

6. Cultivate a lifestyle that enables you to be super focused and eliminate those negative distractions.

PASSION AS A KEY TO SUCCESS

Success is better defined as an achievement of a desired aim or purpose. More than money or fame, most people desire to align their passions with their work while making a sustainable income. People who are passionate about what they do, rather than just "in it for the money," tend to be people who have more positive outlooks and can overcome difficulties through problem-solving. Passion powers the hard work, determination, and creativity that make great accomplishments possible. If you want to be successful, then you have to be determined to learn everything there is to know about your passion and continue to gain knowledge, and know that there is always more to learn. When faced with a challenge, passionate people don't back down. Instead, they see the opportunity to learn, grow, and move through the challenge with grit. Passion is the fuel that inspires and drives people toward specific goals, no matter how unlikely or difficult they might be. It generates the enthusiasm needed to plow through the biggest obstacles and overcome the most intractable challenges. It inspires loyalty, teamwork, hard work, and, eventually, success. Successful people have a daily routine that helps them follow their passion.

Here are a few reasons why passion drives success for those who put it into action.

1. People with passion don't give up easily
2. People with passion perceive obstacles differently. when faced with challenges they don't back down.

3. Passionate people optimize their time. This helps them cultivate a strong work ethic, which often leads to success.
4. Passionate people have a positive attitude. Passionate people aren't afraid to fail. When they do, they don't dwell on the setback. They look at every experience optimistically and continue to approach their craft with a positive mindset.
5. Passionate people stress less
6. Passionate people stay focused. When you enjoy what you do, it's easier to focus on tasks for prolonged periods.

Passionate people are more likely to succeed in what they set out to do. They channel their passion into motivation and focus and perceive difficulties as opportunities rather than challenges. Passion ignites a drive that makes them more inclined to spend most of their time working, which leads them to be regarded as highly successful in their field of work.

How Do You Learn To Find Passion

Learning how to find your passion may not be as easy as it sounds, but it's well worth the effort. However, if you dare to ask "how do I find my passion," imagine the possibilities, and search for what you love, it is not only a possibility but a probability.

How do you go about learning how to find your passion in life?

1. Find your favorite activity. What is your life's purpose? Have you ever thought of pursuing a career in a pastime or activity you enjoyed as a child? You're ahead of the game if you already do something you enjoy.
2. Figure out what you spend hours reading.
3. Ask around. There are likely people you admire in life, and there are things about them that you would like

to replicate in yourself. Go to them if possible, and pick their brain.

4. Give it a shot first. It's reasonable to assess your new idea before diving into it as a vocation as you're wondering how to find your passion. Do it as a pastime or side job initially, so that you can see if it's your true calling.
5. Do as much research as possible. Know as much about your passion as possible.
6. Take time to practice, practice and practice, and as well learn how to focus.

In addition to the suggestions above, be aware of these things that can hold you back from living your passion:

Pessimistic ideas can prevent you from finding your passion in life. They come and go on their own accord. However, what is within our control is how we respond to them. Thoughts like "I can't do that because…" followed by a list of reasons can hold us back as surely as chains, but they aren't real—they are just thoughts.

CONCLUSION

Always dream big, take consistent action, never give up, think positively and most importantly, believe in yourself and your dreams.

Go for what makes you happy and brings out the best in you.

Put in the time to learn how to find your passion, and you will find that your days are more fulfilling and produce more happiness

www.ingramcontent.com/pod-product-compliance
Lightning Source LLC
LaVergne TN
LVHW020545160826
845677LV00015B/4209

* 9 7 9 8 8 4 6 6 0 4 6 2 9 *